poWerwalk

Walking With the Word

1 John 2.6 – "Whoever says he abides in him ought to **walk** in the same way in which he **walked**."

PowerWalk

poWerWalk

Colossians 2.6 – "Therefore, as you received Christ Jesus
the Lord, so **walk** in him…" (ESV)

Name:

Phone:

*If lost, please read my story below and any stories
from the Bible I've read, along with all my thoughts and
then text or call me. I would love to get together for
coffee to discuss what we've read.

How my story with Jesus began

PowerWalk

Why PowerWalk?

Ecclesiastes 12.1 – "Don't let the excitement of youth cause you to forget your Creator. Honor him in your youth before you grow old and say, 'Life is not pleasant anymore.'" (NLT)

PowerWalk aims to build creative discipline in your spiritual life by learning from the successes and failures of others who've walked with God. This happens as you read their story, creatively express your love and devotion to God, and build discipline as a follower. PowerWalk helps you know and walk with your Creator.

PowerWalking

…races you through 192 captivating stories from the Bible. Why? Because we are hard wired for stories and the Bible is a story about God! Each quarter (13 weeks) you'll read and walk through 48 stories from Scripture.

…speeds you up if you fall behind. Life gets crazy for each of us. It allows time to catch up for those days/weeks when we are extra busy. Each week has two days (Sunday and Wednesday) and each quarter (13th week) a full week to catch up. Of course, there is no completion deadline. Just do your best to walk with Jesus each day.

…stretches your creativity as you express your devotion to God. No two people are the same. PowerWalk appeals to your imagination and desire to walk closer with Jesus. You'll read fascinating stories, have opportunity to express your feelings, illustrate scenes, interact with the story and be challenged to live out the stories you just read.

…exercises the disciplines of Scripture reading, prayer, worship, journaling, memorization of Scripture, and note taking.

…walks you through the Bible on a chronological path. That's a fancy way for saying the stories are in the order they happened. So as your story unfolds, you're reading how God's story developed and continues today.

How to Stride Through PowerWalk?

SUNDAY
High Altitude Training

Listen to a worship song prior to attending church. As you listen, make a list of answered prayer and things you are grateful for from the week before.

Psalm 100.4 "Enter with the password: 'Thank you!' Make yourselves at home, talking praise. Thank him. Worship him." (The Message)

Hustle (keeping with the PowerWalk theme) to Church

Hebrews 10.24-25 "Let's see how inventive we can be in encouraging love and helping out, not avoiding worshiping together as some do but spurring each other on, especially as we see the big Day approaching." (The Message)

MONDAY, TUESDAY, THURSDAY, FRIDAY
Load up with Carbs – The Bread of Life

Read through a story that affected someone's walk with God and then express your feelings & thoughts.

Colossians 3.16 "Let the Word of Christ—the Message—have the run of the house. Give it plenty of room in your lives. Instruct and direct one another using good common sense. And sing, sing your hearts out to God!" (The Message)

Write out the memory verse for the week.

Psalm 119.11 "I've banked your promises in the vault of my heart so I won't sin myself bankrupt." (The Message)

Write out any prayer needs for that day.

Philippians 4.6 "Don't fret or worry. Instead of worrying, pray. Let petitions and praises shape your worries into prayers, letting God know your concerns." (The Message)

PowerWalk

WEDNESDAY
Check Your Heart Rate

Express your worship to God through singing, writing, drawing, painting, poetry, playing an instrument, listening, giving, serving, dancing or sharing your faith with someone.

Psalm 95.6 "So come, let us worship: bow before him, on your knees before God, who made us!" (The Message)

Take notes from the message you hear at youth group.

Jeremiah 30.2 "This is what the Lord, the God of Israel, says: 'Write in a book all the words I have spoken to you.'"

*Your group may not meet on Wednesday night. Oh no! *Breathe...* It will be all right. Just take notes on the night your group meets. No one has to know. It will be our little secret.

SATURDAY
Trail Running – Taking your Race off Road

Jog through the Proverbs or Psalms for the day

Proverbs 1.2 "Written down so we'll know how to live well and right, to understand what life means and where it's going." (The Message)

Time to PowerWalk!

My prayer as I walk through God's Word

Help me to

> <u>Understand</u> Your Word,
>
> <u>Live</u> Your Word,
>
> <u>Share</u> Your Word.

Sunday

Listen to a worship song prior to attending church. As you listen, make a list of things you are grateful for from the week before.

Things I'm thankful God did.

Hustle to Church

Monday

Genesis 1 – Chaos to Creation

What does this story tell you about God?

What aspect of God's creation do you enjoy the most? Why?

What's the best thing you've ever created and why did you create it?

Write out your memory verse for the week.

Exodus 20.12 Honor your father and your mother, so that you may live long in the land the LORD your God is giving you.

Things I'm praying about and answered prayers

Tuesday

Genesis 2 – The First Blind Date

What stands out to you from this story?

What do you think Adam's first words to Eve were?

Why did God make Eve?

Write out your memory verse for the week.

Things I'm praying about and answered prayers

Wednesday

Express your worship to God through singing, writing, drawing, painting, poetry, playing an instrument, listening, serving, dancing, giving or sharing your faith with someone.

How I worshipped God today?

Notes from tonight's message

Thursday

Genesis 3 - The First Sin

What are three things you notice from this story?

Why was it so difficult for Adam to say, 'no' to Eve when tempted with the fruit?

Do you think Adam and Eve felt bad about their sin? Why?

Write out your memory verse for the week.

Things I'm praying about and answered prayers

Friday

Genesis 4 - The Original CSI

Why was Cain so angry? (Draw an emoticon of Cain's face)

When were you the angriest at a family member or friend? How did you make it better?

Write a note expressing your forgiveness to this individual. If you haven't already done so take time to restore the relationship.

Write out your memory verse for the week.

Things I'm praying about and answered prayers

Saturday

Jog through the Proverbs or Psalms for the day. Write down or draw an image from what you read.

Psalm 1

Sunday

Listen to a worship song prior to attending church. As you listen, make a list of things you are grateful for from the week before.

Things I'm thankful God did.

Hustle to Church

Monday

Genesis 6.1-22 – Get Your Umbrella!

What did you learn from this story?

Draw a picture of the ark the way you imagine it.

Write out your memory verse for the week.

Deuteronomy 6.5 Love the LORD your God with all your heart and with all your soul and with all your strength.

Things I'm praying about and answered prayers

Tuesday

Genesis 7 – Water...Everywhere

What is the purpose of this story?

What do you believe God wants us to learn from this story?

Write out your memory verse for the week.

Things I'm praying about and answered prayers

Wednesday

Express your worship to God through singing, writing, drawing, painting, poetry, playing an instrument, listening, serving, dancing, giving or sharing your faith with someone.

How I worshipped God today

Notes from tonight's message

Thursday

Genesis 8 – The Flood

What are three things you notice from this story?

What does this story tell you about God?

Write out your memory verse for the week.

Things I'm praying about and answered prayers

Friday

Genesis 11.1-9 - Reaching for the Heavens

What did you notice from this story?

Draw a picture of the tower the way you imagine it.

Write out your memory verse for the week.

Things I'm praying about and answered prayers

Saturday

Jog through the Proverbs or Psalms for the day. Write down or draw an image from what you read.

Proverbs 1

Sunday

Listen to a worship song prior to attending church. As you listen, make a list of things you are grateful for from the week before.

Things I'm thankful God did.

Hustle to Church

Monday

Job 1 - Job Loses His Family

What is the purpose of telling this story?

What did you learn from this story?

Write out your memory verse for the week.

Joshua 1.8 Do not let this Book of the Law depart from your mouth; meditate on it day and night, so that you may be careful to do everything written in it. Then you will be prosperous and successful.

Things I'm praying about and answered prayers

Tuesday

Job 2 - Job Loses His Health

What's something you'll remember from this story?

What advice would you give to the main character?

Write out your memory verse for the week.

Things I'm praying about and answered prayers

Wednesday

Express your worship to God through singing, writing, drawing, painting, poetry, playing an instrument, listening, serving, dancing, giving or sharing your faith with someone.

How I worshipped God today

Notes from tonight's message

Thursday

Job 42 - Job is Restored

What did you discover about God from this story?

How will you attempt to live differently after reading this story?

Write out your memory verse for the week.

Things I'm praying about and answered prayers

Friday

Genesis 13 – Abram's Story Begins

What was the promise God gave to Abram?

Has God ever shared a promise with you? What was it? If not, take a moment and ask him.

Write out your memory verse for the week.

Things I'm praying about and answered prayers

Saturday

Jog through the Proverbs or Psalms for the day. Write out or draw an image from what you read.

Proverbs 2

Sunday

Listen to a worship song prior to attending church. As you listen, make a list of things you are grateful for from the week before.

Things I'm thankful God did.

Hustle to Church

Monday

Genesis 16 - The Birth of Ishmael

What did you think after reading this story?

What do you believe was the purpose of this story?

Write out your memory verse for the week.

Joshua 1.9 Have I not commanded you? Be strong and courageous. Do not be terrified; do not be discouraged, for the LORD your God will be with you wherever you go.

Things I'm praying about and answered prayers

Tuesday

Genesis 18 – Three Visitors Arrive

What did you find most interesting about this story?

What would you ask angels if they visited you?

Write out your memory verse for the week.

Things I'm praying about and answered prayers

Wednesday

Express your worship to God through singing, writing, drawing, painting, poetry, playing an instrument, listening, serving, dancing, giving or sharing your faith with someone.

How I worshipped God today

Notes from tonight's message

Thursday

Genesis 19 - Destruction of Sodom and Gomorrah

What are three things you noticed from this story?

What advice would you give to the main character?

Write out your memory verse for the week.

Things I'm praying about and answered prayers

Friday

Genesis 21 - The Birth of Isaac

What sticks out to you from this story?

What did you learn from this story?

Write out your memory verse for the week.

Things I'm praying about and answered prayers

Saturday

Jog through the Proverbs or Psalms for the day. Write out your thoughts or draw an image from what you read.

Psalm 23

Sunday

Listen to a worship song prior to attending church. As you listen, make a list of things you are grateful for from the week before.

Things I'm thankful God did.

Hustle to Church

Monday

Genesis 22 - A Test of Faith

What is the purpose of this story?

Draw a picture of Abraham placing Isaac on an altar.

Write out your memory verse for the week.

Psalm 19.14 May the words of my mouth and the meditation of my heart be pleasing in your sight, O LORD, my Rock and my Redeemer.

Things I'm praying about and answered prayers

Tuesday

Genesis 24 - True Love!

What did you find most interesting about this story?

What is one way you can apply this story to your life?

What do you want your wedding day to look like?

Write out your memory verse for the week.

Things I'm praying about and answered prayers

Wednesday

Express your worship to God through singing, writing, drawing, painting, poetry, playing an instrument, listening, serving, dancing, giving or sharing your faith with someone.

How I worshipped God today

Notes from tonight's message

Thursday

Genesis 25.27-34 – Soup du jour

What did you like about this story? What did you dislike?

How would you apply the outcome of this story to your life?

Write out your memory verse for the week.

Things I'm praying about and answered prayers

Friday

Genesis 27 - A Hairy Deception

What sticks out to you from this story?

Have you ever been deceived by someone? What was that like?

Write out your memory verse for the week.

Things I'm praying about and answered prayers

Saturday

Jog through the Proverbs or Psalms for the day. Write out your thoughts or draw an image from what you read.

Proverbs 3

Sunday

Listen to a worship song prior to attending church. As you listen, make a list of things you are grateful for from the week before.

Things I'm thankful God did.

Hustle to Church

Monday

Genesis 28.10-22 - Jacob's Dream

What stuck out to you from this story?

What do you think God wants you to do as a result of this story?

Write out your memory verse for the week.

Psalm 34.4 I sought the Lord, and he answered me; he delivered me from all my fears.

Things I'm praying about and answered prayers

Tuesday

Genesis 29 – More Wedding Cake Please

Why do you think there are so many stories about weddings?

What is something you learned from this story?

Write out your memory verse for the week.

Things I'm praying about and answered prayers

Wednesday

Express your worship to God through singing, writing, drawing, painting, poetry, playing an instrument, listening, serving, dancing, giving or sharing your faith with someone.

How I worshipped God today

Notes from tonight's message

Thursday

Genesis 37 - Joseph's Dream

What's something you'll always remember from this story?

What's the strangest dream you've ever had?

Create Joseph's coat and color it in.

Write out your memory verse for the week.

Things I'm praying about and answered prayers

Friday

Genesis 39 – Accused of Rape

What sticks out to you from this story?

How do you feel when you've been falsely accused?

What's something you'll do differently as a result of this story?

Write out your memory verse for the week.

Things I'm praying about and answered prayers

Saturday

Jog through the Proverbs or Psalms for the day. Write out your thoughts or draw an image from what you read.

Proverbs 4

Sunday

Listen to a worship song prior to attending church. As you listen, make a list of things you are grateful for from the week before.

Things I'm thankful God did.

Hustle to Church

Monday

Genesis 40 – Life Behind Bars

What is the purpose of this story?

What do you think God wants you to do as a result of this story?

Sketch a prison cell

Write out your memory verse for the week.

Psalm 37.23 The Lord makes firm the steps of the one who delights in him

Things I'm praying about and answered prayers

Tuesday

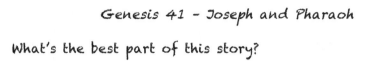

Genesis 41 - Joseph and Pharaoh

What's the best part of this story?

How do you believe this story applies to your life today?

Write out your memory verse for the week.

Things I'm praying about and answered prayers

Wednesday

Express your worship to God through singing, writing, drawing, painting, poetry, playing an instrument, listening, serving, dancing, giving or sharing your faith with someone.

How I worshipped God today

Notes from tonight's message

Thursday

Genesis 42 – Spies in the Land

What are three things you notice from this story?

What do you think God wants you to do as a result of this story?

Write out your memory verse for the week.

Things I'm praying about and answered prayers

PowerWalk

Friday

Genesis 43 – I Love You Bro

What's something you'll always remember from this story?

What does this story tell you about God?

Write out your memory verse for the week.

Things I'm praying about and answered prayers

Saturday

Jog through the Proverbs or Psalms for the day. Write out your thoughts or draw an image from what you read.

Psalm 27

Sunday

Listen to a worship song prior to attending church. As you listen, make a list of things you are grateful for from the week before.

Things I'm thankful God did.

Hustle to Church

Monday

Genesis 44 – Caught With The Goods

Sketch out this scene.

What did you learn from this story?

Write out your memory verse for the week.

Psalm 119:11 I have hidden your word in my heart that I might not sin against you.

Things I'm praying about and answered prayers

Tuesday

Genesis 45 - Forgiveness

What does this story tell you about God?

What's the hardest situation you've ever had to forgive?

Write out your memory verse for the week.

Things I'm praying about and answered prayers

Wednesday

Express your worship to God through singing, writing, drawing, painting, poetry, playing an instrument, listening, serving, dancing, giving or sharing your faith with someone.

How I worshipped God today

Notes from tonight's message

Thursday

Exodus 2 - Float Trip

What are three things you notice from this story?

Draw a picture of Moses floating down the Nile River in a basket.

Write out your memory verse for the week.

Things I'm praying about and answered prayers

Friday

Exodus 3 – The Burning Bush

What did you notice from this story?

What does this story tell you about God?

Draw a picture of Moses next to a burning bush.

Write out your memory verse for the week.

Things I'm praying about and answered prayers

Saturday

Jog through the Proverbs or Psalms for the day. Write out your thoughts or draw an image from what you read.

Proverbs 5

Sunday

Listen to a worship song prior to attending church. As you listen, make a list of things you are grateful for from the week before.

Things I'm thankful God did.

Hustle to Church

Monday

Exodus 5 - Road Trip

What did you like about this story? What did you dislike?

How will you attempt to live differently after reading this story?

Write out your memory verse for the week.

Lamentations 3.25 The Lord is good to those whose hope is in him, to the one who seeks him.

Things I'm praying about and answered prayers

Tuesday

Exodus 6.28-7.13 - Wait...What?

What does this story tell you about God?

Sketch a picture of a staff turning into a snake.

Write out your memory verse for the week.

Things I'm praying about and answered prayers

Wednesday

Express your worship to God through singing, writing, drawing, painting, poetry, playing an instrument, listening, serving, dancing, giving or sharing your faith with someone.

How I worshipped God today

Notes from tonight's message

Thursday

Exodus 7.14-25 – A River of Blood

What are three things you notice from this story?

How do you believe this story applies to your life today?

Write out your memory verse for the week.

Things I'm praying about and answered prayers

Friday

Exodus 8 - The Plagues

What's something you'll always remember from this story?

What does this story tell you about God?

Write out your memory verse for the week.

Things I'm praying about and answered prayers

Saturday

Jog through the Proverbs or Psalms for the day. Write out your thoughts or draw an image from what you read.

Proverbs 6

Sunday

Listen to a worship song prior to attending church. As you listen, make a list of things you are grateful for from the week before.

Things I'm thankful God did.

Hustle to Church

Monday

Exodus 9 - Plagued by Plagues

What makes this a difficult story to understand?

What do you believe God wants you to know about him after reading this story?

Write out your memory verse for the week.

Isaiah 40.31 But those who hope in the LORD will renew their strength. They will soar on wings like eagles; they will run and not grow weary, they will walk and not be faint.

Things I'm praying about and answered prayers

Tuesday

Exodus 10 – A Heart of Stone

What does this story tell you about Pharaoh and his hard heart?

Which plague would you personally hate the most? Why?

Write out your memory verse for the week.

Things I'm praying about and answered prayers

Wednesday

Express your worship to God through singing, writing, drawing, painting, poetry, playing an instrument, listening, serving, dancing, giving or sharing your faith with someone.

How I worshipped God today

Notes from tonight's message

Thursday

Exodus 11 – Crying in the Streets

What are three things you notice from this story?

What do you think God wants you to do as a result of this story?

Write out your memory verse for the week.

Things I'm praying about and answered prayers

Friday

Exodus 12 - The Passover

What's something you'll always remember from this story?

Have you ever been in a situation where you warned someone of danger ahead? What happened?

Write out your memory verse for the week.

Things I'm praying about and answered prayers

Saturday

Jog through the Proverbs or Psalms for the day. Write out your thoughts or draw an image from what you read.

Psalm 34

Sunday

Listen to a worship song prior to attending church. As you listen, make a list of things you are grateful for from the week before.

Things I'm thankful God did.

Hustle to Church

Monday

Exodus 13.17-14.31 - Crossing the Red Sea

What are a few things you notice in this story?

Draw a picture of the Israelites crossing the Red Sea

Write out your memory verse for the week.

Isaiah 41.10 So do not fear, for I am with you; do not be dismayed, for I am your God. I will strengthen you and help you; I will uphold you with my righteous right hand.

Things I'm praying about and answered prayers

Tuesday

Exodus 16 - Manna Burgers

What did you like and dislike about this story?

What's your favorite meal?

Write out your memory verse for the week.

Things I'm praying about and answered prayers

Wednesday

Express your worship to God through singing, writing, drawing, painting, poetry, playing an instrument, listening, serving, dancing, giving or sharing your faith with someone.

How I worshipped God today

Notes from tonight's message

Thursday

Exodus 19 - Moses Receives the Law

What is the purpose of telling this story?

Write out the story in your own words.

Write out your memory verse for the week.

Things I'm praying about and answered prayers

Friday

Exodus 20 - The Ten Commandments

Describe this scene.

Write out the 10 Commandments.

Write out your memory verse for the week.

Things I'm praying about and answered prayers

Saturday

Jog through the Proverbs or Psalms for the day. Write out your thoughts or draw an image from what you read.

Proverbs 7

Sunday

Listen to a worship song prior to attending church. As you listen, make a list of things you are grateful for from the week before.

Things I'm thankful God did.

Hustle to Church

Monday

Exodus 32 – The Golden Calf

What did you most identify with in this story?

Is there an idol in your life you need to destroy? What is it?

Write out your memory verse for the week.

Matthew 5.6 Blessed are those who hunger and thirst for righteousness, for they will be filled.

Things I'm praying about and answered prayers

Tuesday

Numbers 12.1-16 – Miriam and Aaron

What are five words that come to your mind after reading this story?

Have you ever got jealous of someone else? What was the outcome?

Write out your memory verse for the week.

Things I'm praying about and answered prayers

Wednesday

Express your worship to God through singing, writing, drawing, painting, poetry, playing an instrument, listening, serving, dancing, giving or sharing your faith with someone.

How I worshipped God today

Notes from tonight's message

Thursday

Numbers 13 - I Spy Something...

What does this story tell you about God?

Is your personality more like the 10 spies or Joshua and Caleb? Why?

Write out your memory verse for the week.

Things I'm praying about and answered prayers

Friday

Numbers 14 – Uprising!

Describe this scene.

What is your response when following a leader you disagree with?

Write out your memory verse for the week.

Things I'm praying about and answered prayers

PowerWalk

Saturday

Jog through the Proverbs or Psalms for the day. Write out your thoughts or draw an image from what you read.

Proverbs 8

Sunday

Listen to a worship song prior to attending church. As you listen, make a list of things you are grateful for from the week before.

Things I'm thankful God did.

Hustle to Church

*Next week is the last week of the quarter. Take the week to catch up or read through your insights over the past 12 weeks. Congratulations on finishing! You're doing great.

Wednesday

Pray the Lord's Prayer today.

Matthew 6.9-13 - Our Father in heaven, may your name be kept holy. May your Kingdom come soon. May your will be done on earth, as it is in heaven. Give us today the food we need, and forgive us our sins, as we have forgiven those who sin against us. And don't let us yield to temptation, but rescue us from the evil one. (NLT)

Notes from tonight's message

Monday

Numbers 16 – More Rebellion

What was this story all about?

What should our response be when following a leader we disagree with?

Write out your memory verse for the week.

Matthew 5.10 Blessed are those who are persecuted because of righteousness, for theirs is the kingdom of heaven.

Things I'm praying about and answered prayers

Tuesday

Numbers 25 – Immorality

What message did you get from reading this story?

How do you deal with sexual temptation?

Write out your memory verse for the week.

Things I'm praying about and answered prayers

Wednesday

Express your worship to God through singing, writing, drawing, painting, poetry, playing an instrument, listening, serving, dancing, giving or sharing your faith with someone.

How I worshipped God today

Notes from tonight's message

Thursday

Deuteronomy 6 – All In!

What does this story tell you about God?

How do we love God with our heart, soul and strength?

Write out your memory verse for the week.

Things I'm praying about and answered prayers

Friday

Deuteronomy 31 - The Joshua Leader

What just happened?

What qualities does it take to be a leader?

Write out your memory verse for the week.

Things I'm praying about and answered prayers

Saturday

Jog through the Proverbs or Psalms for the day. Write out your thoughts or draw an image from what you read.

Psalm 37

Sunday

Listen to a worship song prior to attending church. As you listen, make a list of things you are grateful for from the week before.

Things I'm thankful God did.

Hustle to Church

Monday

Joshua 2 – The Prostitute and the Spies

What does this story say about God and his love for people?

Draw a picture of Rahab lowering the spies down the wall.

Write out your memory verse for the week.

Matthew 5.16 In the same way, let your light shine before men, that they may see your good deeds and praise your Father in heaven.

Things I'm praying about and answered prayers

Tuesday

Joshua 3 - Crossing the Jordan

Describe what it must have been like to cross the Jordan.

What are some areas of your life you have to cross over and leave behind?

Write out your memory verse for the week.

Things I'm praying about and answered prayers

Wednesday

Express your worship to God through singing, writing, drawing, painting, poetry, playing an instrument, listening, serving, dancing, giving or sharing your faith with someone.

How I worshipped God today

Notes from tonight's message

Thursday

Joshua 6 - Powerwalking Around Jericho

Describe the sounds, smell, sights of this.

What's an area of your life you need for the walls to come down?

Write out your memory verse for the week.

Things I'm praying about and answered prayers

Friday

Joshua 7 – Achan's Sin

What did you most identify with in this story?

What is the danger of trying to hide our sin?

Write out your memory verse for the week.

Things I'm praying about and answered prayers

Saturday

Jog through the Proverbs or Psalms for the day. Write out your thoughts or draw an image from what you read.

Proverbs 9

Sunday

Listen to a worship song prior to attending church. As you listen, make a list of things you are grateful for from the week before.

Things I'm thankful God did.

Hustle to Church

Monday

Joshua 8 - The Attack on Ai

What are a few things you noticed from the story?

What are some of your feelings after reading this story?

Write out your memory verse for the week.

Matthew 7.7 Ask and it will be given to you; seek and you will find; knock and the door will be opened to you.

Things I'm praying about and answered prayers

Tuesday

Joshua 10 - Sun Stands Still

Describe what this scene must have looked like.

Do you feel like God brings victory to your life? Why?

Write out your memory verse for the week.

Things I'm praying about and answered prayers

Wednesday

Express your worship to God through singing, writing, drawing, painting, poetry, playing an instrument, listening, serving, dancing, giving or sharing your faith with someone.

How I worshipped God today

Notes from tonight's message

Thursday

Joshua 23 - Final Instructions

What did you most identify with in this story?

What advice about being a Christian would you give to others?

Write out your memory verse for the week.

Things I'm praying about and answered prayers

Friday

Judges 3.7-31 - Murder in the Palace!

Write out several things you notice in the story.

Why do you think God included this story in the Bible?

Write out your memory verse for the week.

Things I'm praying about and answered prayers

Saturday

Jog through the Proverbs or Psalms for the day. Write out your thoughts or draw an image from what you read.

Proverbs 10

Sunday

Listen to a worship song prior to attending church. As you listen, make a list of things you are grateful for from the week before.

Things I'm thankful God did.

Hustle to Church

Monday

Judges 4 - Women of Courage

What's the best part of this story?

What's the most courageous thing you've done for God?

Write out your memory verse for the week.

Matthew 6:33 But seek first his kingdom and his righteousness, and all these things will be given to you as well.

Things I'm praying about and answered prayers

Tuesday

Judges 6 - Gideon's Call

What do you believe Gideon was thinking during this story?

What would you say to someone who felt inadequate before God?

Write out your memory verse for the week.

Things I'm praying about and answered prayers

Wednesday

Express your worship to God through singing, writing, drawing, painting, poetry, playing an instrument, listening, serving, dancing, giving or sharing your faith with someone.

How I worshipped God today

Notes from tonight's message

Thursday

Judges 7 - Trumpets, Jars and Torches

Describe the noises you would have heard had you been there.

Have you ever thought God asked something strange of you? What was it like?

Write out your memory verse for the week.

Things I'm praying about and answered prayers

Friday

Judges 13 - A Warrior is Born

Write out a few things you picked up on in the story.

For what purpose do you believe God has called you?

Write out your memory verse for the week.

Things I'm praying about and answered prayers

Saturday

Jog through the Proverbs or Psalms for the day. Write out your thoughts or draw an image from what you read.

Psalm 40

Sunday

Listen to a worship song prior to attending church. As you listen, make a list of things you are grateful for from the week before.

Things I'm thankful God did.

Hustle to Church

Monday

Judges 14 – Samson Gets Married

What's something you'll always remember from this story?

Have you ever asked something of your parents that they didn't want you to have? What was the outcome?

Write out your memory verse for the week.

Mark 11.24 Therefore I tell you, whatever you ask for in prayer, believe that you have received it, and it will be yours.

Things I'm praying about and answered prayers

Tuesday

Judges 15 - The Anger of Samson

Why did Samson get so angry? (Draw an emoticon of Samson's face.)

What makes you really angry? How do you deal with anger?

Write out your memory verse for the week.

Things I'm praying about and answered prayers

Wednesday

Express your worship to God through singing, writing, drawing, painting, poetry, playing an instrument, listening, serving, dancing, giving or sharing your faith with someone.

How I worshipped God today

Notes from tonight's message

Thursday

Judges 16 - Samson's First Haircut

What makes this a sad story?

What are the outcomes of disobedience to God?

Write out your memory verse for the week.

Things I'm praying about and answered prayers

Friday

Ruth 1 – Death of Ruth's Husband

Write three things you observed in this story.

What advice would you give to the main character?

Write out your memory verse for the week.

Things I'm praying about and answered prayers

Saturday

Jog through the Proverbs or Psalms for the day. Write out your thoughts or draw an image from what you read.

Proverbs 11

Sunday

Listen to a worship song prior to attending church. As you listen, make a list of things you are grateful for from the week before.

Things I'm thankful God did.

Hustle to Church

PowerWalk

Monday

Ruth 2 – Ruth Meets Boaz

What's something you'll always remember from this story?

What does God want us to learn from this?

Write out your memory verse for the week.

Luke 9.23 Then he said to them all: Whoever wants to be my disciple must deny themselves and take up their cross daily and follow me.

Things I'm praying about and answered prayers

Tuesday

Ruth 3 - Wedding Bells

What's the best part of this story?

What did you learn from this story?

Write out your memory verse for the week.

Things I'm praying about and answered prayers

Wednesday

Express your worship to God through singing, writing, drawing, painting, poetry, playing an instrument, listening, serving, dancing, giving or sharing your faith with someone.

How I worshipped God today

Notes from tonight's message

Thursday

Ruth 4 - Mr and Mrs Boaz

What's something you'll always remember from this story?

What do you believe God is showing us from the story of Ruth?

Write out your memory verse for the week.

Things I'm praying about and answered prayers

Friday

1 Samuel 1 - Hannah Gives Birth

What is the most interesting part of this story?

How will you attempt to live differently after reading this story?

Write out your memory verse for the week.

Things I'm praying about and answered prayers

Saturday

Jog through the Proverbs or Psalms for the day. Write out your thoughts or draw an image from what you read.

Proverbs 12

Sunday

Listen to a worship song prior to attending church. As you listen, make a list of things you are grateful for from the week before.

Things I'm thankful God did.

Hustle to Church

Monday

1 Samuel 2.12-36 – The Bad Boys

What did you notice from this story?

What do you think it means to be dedicated to God?

Write out your memory verse for the week.

John 3.16 For God so loved the world that he gave his one and only Son, that whoever believes in him shall not perish but have eternal life.

Things I'm praying about and answered prayers

Tuesday

1 Samuel 3 – Are You Listening?

List five observations you have from the story.

What is it like to have the Lord speak to you?

Write out your memory verse for the week.

Things I'm praying about and answered prayers

Wednesday

Express your worship to God through singing, writing, drawing, painting, poetry, playing an instrument, listening, serving, dancing, giving or sharing your faith with someone.

How I worshipped God today

Notes from tonight's message

Thursday

1 Samuel 5 - The Ark is Captured

Write the story in your own words.

Sketch out a picture of what you just read.

Write out your memory verse for the week.

Things I'm praying about and answered prayers

Friday

1 Samuel 9 - Donkey Hunting

What do you find interesting about this story?

What did you learn from this story?

Write out your memory verse for the week.

Things I'm praying about and answered prayers

Saturday

Jog through the Proverbs or Psalms for the day. Write out your thoughts or draw an image from what you read.

Psalm 46

Sunday

Listen to a worship song prior to attending church. As you listen, make a list of things you are grateful for from the week before.

Things I'm thankful God did.

Hustle to Church

Monday

1 Samuel 10 - Saul Anointed King

What is something you'll always remember from this story?

What advice would you give to the main character?

Write out your memory verse for the week.

John 5.24 Very truly I tell you, whoever hears my word and believes him who sent me has eternal life and will not be judged but has crossed over from death to life.

Things I'm praying about and answered prayers

Tuesday

1 Samuel 13 - Saul Disobeys God

What is the purpose of this story?

Write about a time you disobeyed God and how you handled it.

Write out your memory verse for the week.

Things I'm praying about and answered prayers

Wednesday

Express your worship to God through singing, writing, drawing, painting, poetry, playing an instrument, listening, serving, dancing, giving or sharing your faith with someone.

How I worshipped God today

Notes from tonight's message

Thursday

1 Samuel 15 - Rebellion

What did you most identify with in this story?

Have you ever disobeyed God because you were afraid of what others would think? What happened?

Write out your memory verse for the week.

Things I'm praying about and answered prayers

Friday

1 Samuel 17 - A Giant Killer

What makes this a great story?

What are some giant things you're facing in your life? How will you go about defeating them?

Write out your memory verse for the week.

Things I'm praying about and answered prayers

Saturday

Jog through the Proverbs or Psalms for the day. Write out your thoughts or draw an image from what you read.

Proverbs 13

Sunday

Listen to a worship song prior to attending church. As you listen, make a list of things you are grateful for from the week before.

Things I'm thankful God did.

Hustle to Church

Monday

1 Samuel 18 - Shish Kebab

How would you tell the story in your own words?

Have you ever had someone really jealous of you? How did you handle it?

Write out your memory verse for the week.

John 14:6 Jesus answered, "I am the way and the truth and the life. No one comes to the Father except through me."

Things I'm praying about and answered prayers

Tuesday

1 Samuel 20 – A Good Friend

What did you learn about David and Jonathan from this story?

What are some things you can do to be a true friend to someone?

Write out your memory verse for the week.

Things I'm praying about and answered prayers

Wednesday

Express your worship to God through singing, writing, drawing, painting, poetry, playing an instrument, listening, serving, dancing, giving or sharing your faith with someone.

How I worshipped God today

Notes from tonight's message

Thursday

1 Samuel 24 - Spared!

What surprises you about this story?

What do you admire about David's character from this story?

Write out your memory verse for the week.

Things I'm praying about and answered prayers

Friday

2 Samuel 1 - Death of a Friend

What's something you'll always remember from this story?

What do you think God wants you to do as a result of this story?

Write out your memory verse for the week.

Things I'm praying about and answered prayers

Saturday

Jog through the Proverbs or Psalms for the day. Write out your thoughts or draw an image from what you read.

Proverbs 14

Sunday

Listen to a worship song prior to attending church. As you listen, make a list of things you are grateful for from the week before.

Things I'm thankful God did.

Hustle to Church

Monday

2 Samuel 6 - David Dances

What did you like about this story?

Have you ever been so excited about Jesus that others thought you a bit crazy? What was that like?

Write out your memory verse for the week.

John 15.7 If you remain in me and my words remain in you, ask whatever you wish, and it will be given you.

Things I'm praying about and answered prayers

Tuesday

2 Samuel 11 - The Cover Up

What did you learn about David from this story?

Describe a time you sinned and how you tried to cover it up

Write out your memory verse for the week.

Things I'm praying about and answered prayers

Wednesday

Express your worship to God through singing, writing, drawing, painting, poetry, playing an instrument, listening, serving, dancing, giving or sharing your faith with someone.

How I worshipped God today

Notes from tonight's message

Thursday

2 Samuel 12 - Caught!

What did David do right once he was caught in his sin?

Describe a time you were caught in sin and how you handled it.

Write out your memory verse for the week.

Things I'm praying about and answered prayers

Friday

2 Samuel 24 – The Census That Didn't Make Sense

What does God want to teach us from this story?

Describe a time in your life when you failed to trust the Lord?

Write out your memory verse for the week.

Things I'm praying about and answered prayers

Saturday

Jog through the Proverbs or Psalms for the day. Write out your thoughts or draw an image from what you read.

Psalm 51

Sunday

Listen to a worship song prior to attending church. As you listen, make a list of things you are grateful for from the week before.

Things I'm thankful God did.

Hustle to Church

Monday

1 Kings 1 - Trouble in the Kingdom

What are a few things you noticed from this story?

What do you believe God wants us to learn from this story?

Write out your memory verse for the week.

Acts 1.8 But you will receive power when the Holy Spirit comes on you; and you will be my witnesses in Jerusalem, and in all Judea and Samaria, and to the ends of the earth.

Things I'm praying about and answered prayers

Tuesday

1 Kings 3 – I Need Some Wisdom

What's the best part of this story?

What is one thing you would ask God for in your life?
Make this a prayer request.

Write out your memory verse for the week.

Things I'm praying about and answered prayers

Wednesday

Express your worship to God through singing, writing, drawing, painting, poetry, playing an instrument, listening, serving, dancing, giving or sharing your faith with someone.

How I worshipped God today

Notes from tonight's message

Thursday

1 Kings 11 – Solomon Turns to Idols

How easy is it for people to turn away from God and follow idols?

What are some idols you deal with in your life?

Write out your memory verse for the week.

Things I'm praying about and answered prayers

Friday

1 Kings 18 – Water, Rocks, Fire and the Power of God

Do you think this story could ever be a movie? Why?

Draw a picture of this scene.

Write out your memory verse for the week.

Things I'm praying about and answered prayers

Saturday

Jog through the Proverbs or Psalms for the day. Write out your thoughts or draw an image from what you read.

Proverbs 15

Sunday

Listen to a worship song prior to attending church. As you listen, make a list of things you are grateful for from the week before.

Things I'm thankful God did.

Hustle to Church

Monday

1 Kings 19 - Down and Out

What are a few things you noticed from this story?

Describe a time when you felt discouraged and far from God. How did you turn it around?

Who is someone you could encourage today? How will you encourage them?

Write out your memory verse for the week.

Acts 4.12 Salvation is found in no one else, for there is no other name under heaven given to mankind by which we must be saved.

Things I'm praying about and answered prayers

Tuesday

2 Kings 2 – Flying First Class

What did you learn from this story?

How will you attempt to live differently after reading this story?

Write out your memory verse for the week.

Things I'm praying about and answered prayers

Wednesday

Express your worship to God through singing, writing, drawing, painting, poetry, playing an instrument, listening, serving, dancing, giving or sharing your faith with someone.

How I worshipped God today

Notes from tonight's message

Thursday

2 Kings 4 - Miracles!

What's something you'll always remember from this story?

What's the greatest miracle you've seen or heard?

Write out your memory verse for the week.

Things I'm praying about and answered prayers

Friday

2 Kings 5 – You Want Me to Do What?

What advice would you have given to Naaman?

How will your life be different after reading this story?

Write out your memory verse for the week.

Things I'm praying about and answered prayers

Saturday

Jog through the Proverbs or Psalms for the day. Write out your thoughts or draw an image from what you read.

Proverbs 16

Sunday

Listen to a worship song prior to attending church. As you listen, make a list of things you are grateful for from the week before.

Things I'm thankful God did.

Hustle to Church

*Next week is the last week of the quarter. Take the week to catch up or read through your insights over the past 12 weeks. Congratulations on finishing! You're doing great.

Wednesday

Pray the Lord's Prayer today.

Matthew 6.9-13 - Our Father in heaven, may your name be kept holy. May your Kingdom come soon. May your will be done on earth, as it is in heaven. Give us today the food we need, and forgive us our sins, as we have forgiven those who sin against us. And don't let us yield to temptation, but rescue us from the evil one. (NLT)

Notes from tonight's message

Monday

Jonah 1 – Running From God

What are some of your observations from this story?

Have you ever tried to run and hide from God? Why?

Write out your memory verse for the week.

Romans 5.8 But God demonstrates his own love for us in this: While we were still sinners, Christ died for us.

Things I'm praying about and answered prayers

Tuesday

Jonah 2 - Sushi!

What do you find most fascinating about this story?

Describe a time you felt separated from God. How did you get close to him again?

Draw a tiny whale.

Write out your memory verse for the week.

Things I'm praying about and answered prayers

Wednesday

Express your worship to God through singing, writing, drawing, painting, poetry, playing an instrument, listening, serving, dancing, giving or sharing your faith with someone.

How I worshipped God today

Notes from tonight's message

Thursday

Jonah 3 - Jonah Has a Message

What's the best part of this story?

Describe a time God called you to share your faith?

Write out your memory verse for the week.

Things I'm praying about and answered prayers

Friday

Jonah 4 - Jonah Gets Angry

Write some of your insights from this story?

Have you ever got angry with God? Why? How did you handle it?

Write out your memory verse for the week.

Things I'm praying about and answered prayers

Saturday

Jog through the Proverbs or Psalms for the day. Write out your thoughts or draw an image from what you read.

Psalm 62

Sunday

Listen to a worship song prior to attending church. As you listen, make a list of things you are grateful for from the week before.

Things I'm thankful God did.

Hustle to Church

Monday

Daniel 3 - Reservations for Four

Write this story in your own words.

Draw a picture of this.

Write out your memory verse for the week.

Romans 6:23 For the wages of sin is death, but the gift of God is eternal life in Christ Jesus our Lord.

Things I'm praying about and answered prayers

Tuesday

Daniel 6 – The First Daniel Fast

What's something you'll never forget from this story?

Describe a time when you had to truly rely on God.

Write out your memory verse for the week.

Things I'm praying about and answered prayers

Wednesday

Express your worship to God through singing, writing, drawing, painting, poetry, playing an instrument, listening, serving, dancing, giving or sharing your faith with someone.

How I worshipped God today

Notes from tonight's message

Thursday

Esther 1 - A Queen Refuses the King's Request

What are three things you notice from this story?

Explain a time when you refused to obey someone and the outcome.

Write out your memory verse for the week.

Things I'm praying about and answered prayers

Friday

Esther 2 - Esther is Chosen

What did you most identify with in this story?

Given your background, what makes it difficult to believe that God would choose you to serve him?

Write out your memory verse for the week.

Things I'm praying about and answered prayers

Saturday

Jog through the Proverbs or Psalms for the day. Write out your thoughts or draw an image from what you read.

Proverbs 17

Sunday

Listen to a worship song prior to attending church. As you listen, make a list of things you are grateful for from the week before.

Things I'm thankful God did.

Hustle to Church

Monday

Esther 3 - Secrets in the Kingdom

What is the purpose of telling this story?

What are some of the injustices you see in our world today? What would you do to turn this around?

Write out your memory verse for the week.

Romans 8.28 And we know that in all things God works for the good of those who love him, who have been called according to his purpose.

Things I'm praying about and answered prayers

Tuesday

Esther 4 – We Need Your Help

What did you most identify with in this story?

Why do you believe God has chosen you for this time in history?

Write out your memory verse for the week.

Things I'm praying about and answered prayers

Wednesday

Express your worship to God through singing, writing, drawing, painting, poetry, playing an instrument, listening, serving, dancing, giving or sharing your faith with someone.

How I worshipped God today

Notes from tonight's message

Thursday

Esther 5 – Standing Before the King

List some of your observations from this story?

Have you ever come before King Jesus to stand up for others? Explain.

Write out your memory verse for the week.

Things I'm praying about and answered prayers

Friday

Esther 6 - Mordecai is Honored

What stands out to you most from this story?

What are some things you can do to honor others?

Write out your memory verse for the week.

Things I'm praying about and answered prayers

Saturday

Jog through the Proverbs or Psalms for the day. Write out your thoughts or draw an image from what you read.

Proverbs 18

Sunday

Listen to a worship song prior to attending church. As you listen, make a list of things you are grateful for from the week before.

Things I'm thankful God did.

Hustle to Church

Monday

Esther 7 - The Hanging

What's something you'll always remember from this story?

How do you love your enemies?

Write out your memory verse for the week.

Romans 10.9 That if you confess with your mouth, "Jesus is Lord," and believe in your heart that God raised him from the dead, you will be saved.

Things I'm praying about and answered prayers

Tuesday

Esther 8 - Pleading Before the King

What did you like about this story? What did you dislike?

What is one need you see in our world today? What can you do to help change this?

Write out your memory verse for the week.

Things I'm praying about and answered prayers

Wednesday

Express your worship to God through singing, writing, drawing, painting, poetry, playing an instrument, listening, serving, dancing, giving or sharing your faith with someone.

How I worshipped God today

Notes from tonight's message

Thursday

Nehemiah 1 - Bad News

How did Nehemiah handle the bad news?

How do you respond when you hear bad news?

Write out your memory verse for the week.

Things I'm praying about and answered prayers

Friday

Nehemiah 2 - Road Trip

What's the best part of this story?

Where do you believe God is calling you? How are you preparing yourself for this call?

Write out your memory verse for the week.

Things I'm praying about and answered prayers

Saturday

Jog through the Proverbs or Psalms for the day. Write out your thoughts or draw an image from what you read.

Psalm 69

Sunday

Listen to a worship song prior to attending church. As you listen, make a list of things you are grateful for from the week before.

Things I'm thankful God did.

Hustle to Church

Monday

Nehemiah 3 - Rebuilding the Wall

What's the best part of this story?

Do you feel God is calling you to rebuild something in your life that the enemy has torn down? What are you doing to rebuild?

Write out your memory verse for the week.

Romans 12.2 Do not conform any longer to the pattern of this world, but be transformed by the renewing of your mind. Then you will be able to test and approve what God's will is — his good, pleasing and perfect will.

Things I'm praying about and answered prayers

Tuesday

Nehemiah 4 - Opposition

What five words come to mind after reading this story?

How do you handle opposition?

Write out your memory verse for the week.

Things I'm praying about and answered prayers

Wednesday

Express your worship to God through singing, writing, drawing, painting, poetry, playing an instrument, listening, serving, dancing, giving or sharing your faith with someone.

How I worshipped God today

Notes from tonight's message

Thursday

Nehemiah 5 - Helping the Poor

What did you like about this story? What did you dislike?

What are some ways you are helping or would like to help the poor?

Write out your memory verse for the week.

Things I'm praying about and answered prayers

Friday

Luke 1.1-56 Angels Everywhere

What's the best part of this story?

What is God birthing (doing) in you?

Write out your memory verse for the week.

Things I'm praying about and answered prayers

Saturday

Jog through the Proverbs or Psalms for the day. Write out your thoughts or draw an image from what you read.

Proverbs 19

Sunday

Listen to a worship song prior to attending church. As you listen, make a list of things you are grateful for from the week before.

Things I'm thankful God did.

Hustle to Church

Monday

Luke 1.57-80 Welcome! John the Baptist

What are a few things you notice about John?

What were the circumstances around your birth? How does this affect you today?

Write out your memory verse for the week.

1 Corinthians 10:13 No temptation has seized you except what is common to man. And God is faithful; he will not let you be tempted beyond what you can bear. But when you are tempted, he will also provide a way out, so that you can stand up under it.

Things I'm praying about and answered prayers

Tuesday

Luke 2.1-20 – A King is Born

Write this story in your own words.

How did Jesus birth, life, death and resurrection change your life?

Write out your memory verse for the week.

Things I'm praying about and answered prayers

Wednesday

Express your worship to God through singing, writing, drawing, painting, poetry, playing an instrument, listening, serving, dancing, giving or sharing your faith with someone.

How I worshipped God today

Notes from tonight's message

Thursday

Matthew 2.1-23 – What's a Magi?

What do you believe is the purpose for this story?

What was the best Christmas gift you ever received? Ever gave?

Write out your memory verse for the week.

Things I'm praying about and answered prayers

Friday

Luke 2.21-52 – He's Growing Up Fast

What did you learn from this story?

Do you believe God could use you in your teen years? Why?

Write out your memory verse for the week.

Things I'm praying about and answered prayers

Saturday

Jog through the Proverbs or Psalms for the day. Write out your thoughts or draw an image from what you read.

Proverbs 20

Sunday

Listen to a worship song prior to attending church. As you listen, make a list of things you are grateful for from the week before.

Things I'm thankful God did.

Hustle to Church

Monday

Luke 4.1-13 - Temptation

How did Jesus handle temptation?

What is the greatest temptation you deal with? How do you deal with it?

Write out your memory verse for the week.

2 Corinthians 5:17 Therefore, if anyone is in Christ he is a new creation; the old has gone, the new has come!

Things I'm praying about and answered prayers

Tuesday

John 1.35-51 - The First Power Walkers

What stands out to you from this story?

Describe the moment you made the decision to follow Jesus.

Write out your memory verse for the week.

Things I'm praying about and answered prayers

Wednesday

Express your worship to God through singing, writing, drawing, painting, poetry, playing an instrument, listening, serving, dancing, giving or sharing your faith with someone.

How I worshipped God today

Notes from tonight's message

Thursday

John 2.1-11 - Water into Wine

Describe what this wedding must have felt like to the people?

What miracle do you need Jesus to do in your life? Take a moment to ask him and then make it a matter of prayer in your life.

Write out your memory verse for the week.

Things I'm praying about and answered prayers

Friday

John 4.1.26 – She Was Married Five Times!

What did you learn about Jesus from this story?

Draw an emoticon of the woman's face following her meeting Jesus.

Describe a time when you told someone about Jesus.

Write out your memory verse for the week.

Things I'm praying about and answered prayers

Saturday

Jog through the Proverbs or Psalms for the day.
Write out your thoughts or draw an image from what
you read.

Psalm 84

Sunday

Listen to a worship song prior to attending church.
As you listen, make a list of things you are grateful for
from the week before.

Things I'm thankful God did.

Hustle to Church

Monday

Mark 1.29-45 - Sick of Being Sick

What's something you'll always remember from this story?

Have you ever prayed for someone to be healed? Describe it.

Write out your memory verse for the week.

2 Corinthians 12:9 But he said to me, "My grace is sufficient for you, for my power is made perfect in weakness." Therefore I will boast all the more gladly about my weaknesses, so that Christ's power may rest on me.

Things I'm praying about and answered prayers

Tuesday

Mark 2.1-12 - Jesus Heals a Paralytic

List five things you noticed from this story?

What's the craziest thing you did to help someone?

Write out your memory verse for the week.

Things I'm praying about and answered prayers

Wednesday

Express your worship to God through singing, writing, drawing, painting, poetry, playing an instrument, listening, serving, dancing, giving or sharing your faith with someone.

How I worshipped God today

Notes from tonight's message

Thursday

Mark 3.1-6 - Uh Oh!

Describe what this story tells others about Jesus.

Have you ever prayed for someone in church? What happened?

Write out your memory verse for the week.

Things I'm praying about and answered prayers

Friday

Matthew 5 – The Sermon

What verses stand out to you from this story?

Draw a picture of Jesus speaking to the multitudes on a mountainside.

Write out your memory verse for the week.

Things I'm praying about and answered prayers

Saturday

Jog through the Proverbs or Psalms for the day. Write out your thoughts or draw an image from what you read.

Proverbs 21

Sunday

Listen to a worship song prior to attending church. As you listen, make a list of things you are grateful for from the week before.

Things I'm thankful God did.

Hustle to Church

Monday

Matthew 6 - Listening to Jesus

What are some of the sights, sounds and smells one would notice from sitting on the hillside listening to Jesus?

What is one verse that stands out to you? Why?

Write out your memory verse for the week.

Galatians 2.20 I have been crucified with Christ and I no longer live, but Christ lives in me. The life I live in the body, I live by faith in the Son of God, who loved me and gave himself for me.

Things I'm praying about and answered prayers

Tuesday

Matthew 7 – Mountaintop Preaching

What are several things you learned from this story?

Which verse is the hardest for you to live? Why?

Write out your memory verse for the week.

Things I'm praying about and answered prayers

Wednesday

Express your worship to God through singing, writing, drawing, painting, poetry, playing an instrument, listening, serving, dancing, giving or sharing your faith with someone.

How I worshipped God today

Notes from tonight's message

Thursday

Luke 7.1-17 - A Centurion and a Widow

What will you always remember from this story?

Describe the similarities you see in these stories.

Write out your memory verse for the week.

Things I'm praying about and answered prayers

Friday

Luke 7.36-50 - Woman Anoints Jesus' Feet

What makes this story so fascinating?

Draw a picture of a woman anointing Jesus' feet. Tape one of your hairs on this page.

Write out your memory verse for the week.

Things I'm praying about and answered prayers

Saturday

Jog through the Proverbs or Psalms for the day. Write out your thoughts or draw an image from what you read.

Proverbs 22

Sunday

Listen to a worship song prior to attending church. As you listen, make a list of things you are grateful for from the week before.

Things I'm thankful God did.

Hustle to Church

Monday

Matthew 13 - Story Time

What are some of the things Jesus in communicating to us in this parables?

Write your own parable (story).

Write out your memory verse for the week.

Ephesians 2.8 For it is by grace you have been saved, through faith — and this not from yourselves, it is the gift of God.

Things I'm praying about and answered prayers

Tuesday

Mark 4.35-41 - Seasick

What is the point of this story?

Draw this scene.

Write out your memory verse for the week.

Things I'm praying about and answered prayers

Wednesday

Express your worship to God through singing, writing, drawing, painting, poetry, playing an instrument, listening, serving, dancing, giving or sharing your faith with someone.

How I worshipped God today

Notes from tonight's message

Thursday

Mark 5 - Demon Guy, Sick Woman and Dead Girl

List several things you notice from these stories.

Describe the similarities you see in these stories.

Write out your memory verse for the week.

Things I'm praying about and answered prayers

Friday

John 5.1-15 - Get in the Pool

Write the story in your own words.

What excuses do we offer to Jesus at times?

Write out your memory verse for the week.

Things I'm praying about and answered prayers

Saturday

Jog through the Proverbs or Psalms for the day. Write out your thoughts or draw an image from what you read.

Psalm 91

Sunday

Listen to a worship song prior to attending church. As you listen, make a list of things you are grateful for from the week before.

Things I'm thankful God did.

Hustle to Church

Monday

Matthew 10 - 24 Feet Go Power Walking!

What are some things Jesus told the disciples?

Where do you believe God is sending you? How are you responding?

Write out your memory verse for the week.

Ephesians 2.10 For we are God's workmanship, created in Christ Jesus to do good works, which God prepared in advance for us to do.

Things I'm praying about and answered prayers

Tuesday

Mark 6.14-29 -Beheaded!

What stands out to you from this story?

Describe a time when being faithful to God cost you something?

Write out your memory verse for the week.

Things I'm praying about and answered prayers

Wednesday

Express your worship to God through singing, writing, drawing, painting, poetry, playing an instrument, listening, serving, dancing, giving or sharing your faith with someone.

How I worshipped God today

Notes from tonight's message

Thursday

Mark 6.30-44 - Reservations for 5000!

Describe what you would have felt/seen if you were the 5000th person to be fed?

What does this story tell you about Jesus?

Write out your memory verse for the week.

Things I'm praying about and answered prayers

Friday

Mark 6.45-56 – Surfing Without a Board

What would your response have been had you seen Jesus walking on water?

Illustrate this scene.

Write out your memory verse for the week.

Things I'm praying about and answered prayers

Saturday

Jog through the Proverbs or Psalms for the day. Write out your thoughts or draw an image from what you read.

Proverbs 23

Sunday

Listen to a worship song prior to attending church. As you listen, make a list of things you are grateful for from the week before.

Things I'm thankful God did.

Hustle to Church

Monday

Mark 7.31-37 - Jesus Heals Deaf Man

What do you like about this story?

Do you believe God still heals today? Why?

Write out your memory verse for the week.

Ephesians 4.32 Be kind and compassionate to one another, forgiving each other, just as in Christ God forgave you.

Things I'm praying about and answered prayers

Tuesday

Mark 8.1-10 - I'm Hungry

Describe what you would have felt/seen if you were the first person to be fed?

How are you helping people who are in need of food and water? How could you help?

Write out your memory verse for the week.

Things I'm praying about and answered prayers

Wednesday

Express your worship to God through singing, writing, drawing, painting, poetry, playing an instrument, listening, serving, dancing, giving or sharing your faith with someone.

How I worshipped God today

Notes from tonight's message

Thursday

Mark 8.31-38 – Jesus Predicts His Death

What does Jesus say we must do to be a follower?

What do you think it means to pick up your cross?

Write out your memory verse for the week.

Things I'm praying about and answered prayers

Friday

> *Mark 9.2-13 - Transfigured? Go Figure.*

Describe what this scene must have looked/felt like?

Describe a time when you felt close to Jesus.

Write out your memory verse for the week.

Things I'm praying about and answered prayers

Saturday

Jog through the Proverbs or Psalms for the day. Write out your thoughts or draw an image from what you read.

Proverbs 24

Sunday

Listen to a worship song prior to attending church. As you listen, make a list of things you are grateful for from the week before.

Things I'm thankful God did.

Hustle to Church

*Next week is the last week of the quarter. Take the week to catch up or read through your insights over the past 12 weeks. Congratulations on finishing! You're doing great.

Wednesday

Pray the Lord's Prayer today.

Matthew 6.9-13 - Our Father in heaven, may your name be kept holy. May your Kingdom come soon. May your will be done on earth, as it is in heaven. Give us today the food we need, and forgive us our sins, as we have forgiven those who sin against us. And don't let us yield to temptation, but rescue us from the evil one. (NLT)

Notes from tonight's message

Monday

Mark 9.14-32 - Jesus Heals a Boy

What did you enjoy about this story?

How can you apply this story to your life?

Write out your memory verse for the week.

Philippians 1.6 Being confident of this, that he who began a good work in you will carry it on to completion until the day of Christ Jesus.

Things I'm praying about and answered prayers

Tuesday

Matthew 18.21-35 - Seventy Times Seven

What did you learn from this story?

Have you ever had a tough time forgiving someone? What did you do to be able to forgive?

Write out your memory verse for the week.

Things I'm praying about and answered prayers

Wednesday

Express your worship to God through singing, writing, drawing, painting, poetry, playing an instrument, listening, serving, dancing, giving or sharing your faith with someone.

How I worshipped God today

Notes from tonight's message

Thursday

Luke 10.1-20 - 72 on Mission

What would it have been like to be one of the 72?

What is something you can do as a result of this story?

Write out your memory verse for the week.

Things I'm praying about and answered prayers

Friday

Luke 11.1-12 - Teach Me To Pray

Write out the Lord's prayer in your own words.

How important is prayer to you?

Write out your memory verse for the week.

Things I'm praying about and answered prayers

Saturday

Jog through the Proverbs or Psalms for the day. Write out your thoughts or draw an image from what you read.

Psalm 116

Sunday

Listen to a worship song prior to attending church. As you listen, make a list of things you are grateful for from the week before.

Things I'm thankful God did.

Hustle to Church

Monday

Luke 15 - Prodigal Son

What does this story say about God?

Which son do you identify with more? Why?

Write out your memory verse for the week.

Philippines 4.6 Do not be anxious about anything, but in everything, by prayer and petition, with thanksgiving, present your requests to God.

Things I'm praying about and answered prayers

Tuesday

Luke 16.19-31 - The Rich Man and Lazarus

What is the point of this story?

Does this change your thoughts about telling others about the gift of salvation? How?

Write out your memory verse for the week.

Things I'm praying about and answered prayers

Wednesday

Express your worship to God through singing, writing, drawing, painting, poetry, playing an instrument, listening, serving, dancing, giving or sharing your faith with someone.

How I worshipped God today

Notes from tonight's message

Thursday

Luke 18.1-14 - Jesus Teaches on Prayer

What's something you'll always remember from this story?

What is prayer? Write out your thoughts.

Write out your memory verse for the week.

Things I'm praying about and answered prayers

Friday

John 8.1-11 - Caught in the Act!

What did you learn about the character of Jesus from this story?

What's the worst sin you've been caught in? How did you handle it?

Write out your memory verse for the week.

Things I'm praying about and answered prayers

Saturday

Jog through the Proverbs or Psalms for the day. Write out your thoughts or draw an image from what you read.

Proverbs 25

Sunday

Listen to a worship song prior to attending church. As you listen, make a list of things you are grateful for from the week before.

Things I'm thankful God did.

Hustle to Church

PowerWalk

Monday

John 9.1-34 - A Man Born Blind

What do you find to be the most fantastic part of this story?

How will you attempt to live differently after reading this story?

Write out your memory verse for the week.

Philippines 4.8 Finally, brothers, whatever is true, whatever is noble, whatever is right, whatever is pure, whatever is lovely, whatever is admirable — if anything is excellent or praiseworthy — think about such things.

Things I'm praying about and answered prayers

Tuesday

John 10.1-21 - The Good Shepherd

What did you learn from this?

Have you ever had a difficult time hearing God's voice?
What did you do?

Write out your memory verse for the week.

Things I'm praying about and answered prayers

Wednesday

Express your worship to God through singing, writing, drawing, painting, poetry, playing an instrument, listening, serving, dancing, giving or sharing your faith with someone.

How I worshipped God today

Notes from tonight's message

Thursday

Matthew 20.1-16 - Parable of the Vineyard Workers

What is the purpose of telling this story?

How will you apply this parable to your life?

Write out your memory verse for the week.

Things I'm praying about and answered prayers

Friday

John 11.17-57 - He Stinks!

What did you find most fascinating about this story?

Sketch a picture of this.

Write out your memory verse for the week.

Things I'm praying about and answered prayers

Saturday

Jog through the Proverbs or Psalms for the day. Write out your thoughts or draw an image from what you read.

Proverbs 26

Sunday

Listen to a worship song prior to attending church. As you listen, make a list of things you are grateful for from the week before.

Things I'm thankful God did.

Hustle to Church

Monday

Luke 18.35-43 - I Can See!

Write this story in your own words.

Have you ever had a difficult time seeing God move in your life? What did you do?

Write out your memory verse for the week.

Colossians 3:23 Whatever you do, work at it with all your heart, as working for the Lord, not for men.

Things I'm praying about and answered prayers

Tuesday

Luke 19.1-10 - Get Out of the Tree

What did you learn from this?

What are the differences between the story from yesterday of the blind man in Luke 18.35-43 and today's story?

Write out your memory verse for the week.

Things I'm praying about and answered prayers

Wednesday

Express your worship to God through singing, writing, drawing, painting, poetry, playing an instrument, listening, serving, dancing, giving or sharing your faith with someone.

How I worshipped God today

Notes from tonight's message

Thursday

Matthew 21.1-11 - Jesus Enter Jerusalem

What is going on in this story?

How could you welcome Jesus onto your campus or in your community?

Write out your memory verse for the week.

Things I'm praying about and answered prayers

Friday

Matthew 22.1-14 – A Feast for a King?

What do you see happening?

How can you apply this story to your life?

Write out your memory verse for the week.

Things I'm praying about and answered prayers

Saturday

Jog through the Proverbs or Psalms for the day. Write out your thoughts or draw an image from what you read.

Psalm 121

Sunday

Listen to a worship song prior to attending church. As you listen, make a list of things you are grateful for from the week before.

Things I'm thankful God did.

Hustle to Church

Monday

Luke 10.29-37 - Good Samaritan

What are three things you see in this story?

Describe a time when you helped someone who was in trouble.

Write out your memory verse for the week.

2 Thessalonians 3.3 But the Lord is faithful, and he will strengthen you and protect you from the evil one.

Things I'm praying about and answered prayers

Tuesday

Matthew 24 – Are You Ready?

List as many signs as you can marking the end times.

What signs of Jesus' return do you see happening today?

Write out your memory verse for the week.

Things I'm praying about and answered prayers

Wednesday

Express your worship to God through singing, writing, drawing, painting, poetry, playing an instrument, listening, serving, dancing, giving or sharing your faith with someone.

How I worshipped God today

Notes from tonight's message

Thursday

Matthew 25.1-13 - 10 Virgins

What is this parable all about?

How does this parable affect your life?

Write out your memory verse for the week.

Things I'm praying about and answered prayers

Friday

Matthew 25-14-30 - You've Got Talent

What principles do you see at work here?

Does this motivate you to work harder for God? Why?

Write out your memory verse for the week.

Things I'm praying about and answered prayers

Saturday

Jog through the Proverbs or Psalms for the day. Write out your thoughts or draw an image from what you read.

Proverbs 27

Sunday

Listen to a worship song prior to attending church. As you listen, make a list of things you are grateful for from the week before.

Things I'm thankful God did.

Hustle to Church

Monday

Matthew 25.31-46 - The Sheep and Goats

What does this show you about God and his compassion for people?

What are five ways you can help others?

Write out your memory verse for the week.

Hebrews 4:16 Let us then approach the throne of grace with confidence, so that we may receive mercy and find grace to help us in our time of need.

Things I'm praying about and answered prayers

Tuesday

Mark 14.1-11 – Waste or Worship?

What did you like about this story?

How does this affect you as a worshipper of God?

Write out your memory verse for the week.

Things I'm praying about and answered prayers

Wednesday

Express your worship to God through singing, writing, drawing, painting, poetry, playing an instrument, listening, serving, dancing, giving or sharing your faith with someone.

How I worshipped God today

Notes from tonight's message

Thursday

John 13.1-20 - 24 Feet To Go

What did this tell you about Jesus?

How does this act by Jesus affect your life as a follower?

Write out your memory verse for the week.

Things I'm praying about and answered prayers

Friday

Mark 14.22-26 - The Lord's Supper

What does the bread and juice represent?

What does the Lord's Supper mean to you? Consider taking communion.

Write out your memory verse for the week.

Things I'm praying about and answered prayers

Saturday

Jog through the Proverbs or Psalms for the day.
Write out your thoughts or draw an image from what
you read.

Proverbs 28

Sunday

Listen to a worship song prior to attending church.
As you listen, make a list of things you are grateful for
from the week before.

Things I'm thankful God did.

Hustle to Church

Monday

Mark 14.32-52 - A Kiss From a Friend

What observations do you read from this story?

Draw a picture of the Garden of Gethsemene as you imagine it.

Write out your memory verse for the week.

Hebrews 11.6 And without faith it is impossible to please God, because anyone who comes to him must believe that he exists and that he rewards those who earnestly seek him.

Things I'm praying about and answered prayers

Tuesday

Mark 14.53-72 – A Rigged Trial

What did you notice from this story?

How does this story apply to your life?

Write out your memory verse for the week.

Things I'm praying about and answered prayers

Wednesday

Express your worship to God through singing, writing, drawing, painting, poetry, playing an instrument, listening, serving, dancing, giving or sharing your faith with someone.

How I worshipped God today

Notes from tonight's message

Thursday

Mark 15 – Jesus' Trial, Crucifixion and Burial

Write what happened in your own words.

How does this affect how you look at Jesus?

Write out your memory verse for the week.

Things I'm praying about and answered prayers

Friday

John 20.1-13 – The Resurrection

Write out a few observations.

Draw a picture of the empty tomb.

Write out your memory verse for the week.

Things I'm praying about and answered prayers

Saturday

Jog through the Proverbs or Psalms for the day. Write out your thoughts or draw an image from what you read.

Psalm 138

Sunday

Listen to a worship song prior to attending church. As you listen, make a list of things you are grateful for from the week before.

Things I'm thankful God did.

Hustle to Church

Monday

Luke 24-13-53 - A Ghost?

How do you think you would have responded if you were with the disciples?

How has walking with Jesus changed your life?

Write out your memory verse for the week.

James 1:22 Do not merely listen to the word, and so deceive yourselves. Do what it says.

Things I'm praying about and answered prayers

Tuesday

John 21 - Breakfast on the Beach

What are a few things that stand out to you?

What does this story tell you about Jesus?

What's your favorite breakfast meal?

Write out your memory verse for the week.

Things I'm praying about and answered prayers

Wednesday

Express your worship to God through singing, writing, drawing, painting, poetry, playing an instrument, listening, serving, dancing, giving or sharing your faith with someone.

How I worshipped God today

Notes from tonight's message

Thursday

Acts 2 – Power in Their Walk

Describe what this day must have looked like to people watching.

Has walking in the Spirit changed you in any way? How so?

Write out your memory verse for the week.

Things I'm praying about and answered prayers

Friday

Acts 3 – A Cripple Now Powerwalking!

What would you have done if you were watching this take place?

How has Jesus helped you walk as a follower?

Write out your memory verse for the week.

Things I'm praying about and answered prayers

Saturday

Jog through the Proverbs or Psalms for the day. Write out your thoughts or draw an image from what you read.

Proverbs 29

Sunday

Listen to a worship song prior to attending church. As you listen, make a list of things you are grateful for from the week before.

Things I'm thankful God did.

Hustle to Church

Monday

Acts 4 – A Night in Jail

List five observations you see in this story.

Have you ever been persecuted for your faith? What was that like?

Write out your memory verse for the week.

James 5:16 Therefore confess your sins to each other and pray for each other so that you may be healed. The prayer of a righteous man is powerful and effective.

Things I'm praying about and answered prayers

Tuesday

Acts 5.1-16 – Ananias and Sapphira

What did you like and dislike about this story?

How did this story affect you?

Write out your memory verse for the week.

Things I'm praying about and answered prayers

Wednesday

Express your worship to God through singing, writing, drawing, painting, poetry, playing an instrument, listening, serving, dancing, giving or sharing your faith with someone.

How I worshipped God today

Notes from tonight's message

Thursday

Act 5.17-42 - Apostles Are Persecuted

What did you most identify with in this story?

Does persecution make you stronger in your faith or weaken it? Why?

Write out your memory verse for the week.

Things I'm praying about and answered prayers

Friday

Acts 7 - Stoning of Stephen

What do you notice about how Stephen handled this episode?

Is your faith strong enough to endure harsh persecution or even dying for your faith? Why?

Write out your memory verse for the week.

Things I'm praying about and answered prayers

Saturday

Jog through the Proverbs or Psalms for the day. Write out your thoughts or draw an image from what you read.

Proverbs 30

Sunday

Listen to a worship song prior to attending church. As you listen, make a list of things you are grateful for from the week before.

Things I'm thankful God did.

Hustle to Church

Monday

Acts 8 – Greater Persecution for the Church

Why do you think the early Church experience so much persecution?

Write out a prayer for Christians who are being persecuted today.

Write out your memory verse for the week.

1 Peter 5.10 And the God of all grace, who called you to his eternal glory in Christ, after you have suffered a little while, will himself restore you and make you strong, firm and steadfast.

Things I'm praying about and answered prayers

Tuesday

Acts 9.1-31 – I Fell Off My Horse

What did you most identify with in this story?

What were you doing right before you met Jesus?

Write out your memory verse for the week.

Things I'm praying about and answered prayers

Wednesday

Express your worship to God through singing, writing, drawing, painting, poetry, playing an instrument, listening, serving, dancing, giving or sharing your faith with someone.

How I worshipped God today

Notes from tonight's message

Thursday

Acts 9.32-43 - Eyes of Compassion

What was the best part of these stories?

How does reading stories about healing increase your faith to pray for others?

Write out your memory verse for the week.

Things I'm praying about and answered prayers

Friday

Acts 12 – The Great Escape

Do you think things like the story you just read happen today? Why?

How did reading this encourage you in your walk with Christ?

Write out your memory verse for the week.

Things I'm praying about and answered prayers

Saturday

Jog through the Proverbs or Psalms for the day. Write out your thoughts or draw an image from what you read.

Psalm 139

Sunday

Listen to a worship song prior to attending church. As you listen, make a list of things you are grateful for from the week before.

Things I'm thankful God did.

Hustle to Church

Monday

Acts 16.16-40 - Behind Bars

Things you noticed?

Put yourself in Paul's sandals. What would you do?

Write out your memory verse for the week.

1 John 1:9 If we confess our sins, he is faithful and just and will forgive us our sins and purify us from all unrighteousness.

Things I'm praying about and answered prayers

Tuesday

Acts 19 – Paul in Ephesus

What do you find most fascinating about this story?

Do you believe God would ever call you to another country to share the gospel? If so, what country? If not, why not?

Write out your memory verse for the week.

Things I'm praying about and answered prayers

Wednesday

Express your worship to God through singing, writing, drawing, painting, poetry, playing an instrument, listening, serving, dancing, giving or sharing your faith with someone.

How I worshipped God today

Notes from tonight's message

Thursday

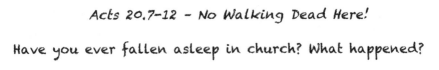

Acts 20.7-12 - No Walking Dead Here!

Have you ever fallen asleep in church? What happened?

How will your life be different after reading this story?

Write out your memory verse for the week.

Things I'm praying about and answered prayers

Friday

Acts 21.37-22.30 – Paul's Story

Why is it so important we share our story with others?

List five people you plan on sharing your story of faith with in the near future.

Write out your memory verse for the week.

Things I'm praying about and answered prayers

Saturday

Jog through the Proverbs or Psalms for the day. Write out your thoughts or draw an image from what you read.

Proverbs 31

Sunday

Listen to a worship song prior to attending church. As you listen, make a list of things you are grateful for from the week before.

Things I'm thankful God did.

Hustle to Church

PowerWalk

Monday

Acts 27 - Shipwrecked!

What did you learn about the life of Paul from this story?

Why do you think bad things happen to people God has called?

Write out your memory verse for the week.

Revelation 3.20 Here I am! I stand at the door and knock. If anyone hears my voice and opens the door, I will come in and eat with that person, and they with me.

Things I'm praying about and answered prayers

Tuesday

Acts 28 – Final Journey

What do you find most fascinating about this story?

Write out how you want your life to be remembered by others.

Write out your memory verse for the week.

Things I'm praying about and answered prayers

Wednesday

Express your worship to God through singing, writing, drawing, painting, poetry, playing an instrument, listening, serving, dancing, giving or sharing your faith with someone.

How I worshipped God today

Notes from tonight's message

Thursday

Revelation 1 – Banished!

What do you think it would be like to be sent to an island to spend the rest of your life?

Write how you think you would respond if you saw Jesus standing in front of you.

Write out your memory verse for the week.

Things I'm praying about and answered prayers

Friday

Revelation 21 - New Heaven and Earth

What is heaven and earth going to be like in the future?

What do you think it will be like to live in heaven for eternity?

Draw an emoji of someone's first moments in heaven.

Write out your memory verse for the week.

Things I'm praying about and answered prayers

Saturday

Jog through the Proverbs or Psalms for the day. Write out your thoughts or draw an image from what you read.

Psalm 150

Sunday

Listen to a worship song prior to attending church. As you listen, make a list of things you are grateful for from the week before.

Things I'm thankful God did.

Hustle to Church

*Next week is the last week of the quarter. Take the week to catch up or read through your insights over the past 12 weeks. Congratulations on finishing!

Wednesday

Pray the Lord's Prayer today.

Matthew 6.9-13 - Our Father in heaven, may your name be kept holy. May your Kingdom come soon. May your will be done on earth, as it is in heaven. Give us today the food we need, and forgive us our sins, as we have forgiven those who sin against us. And don't let us yield to temptation, but rescue us from the evil one. (NLT)

Notes from tonight's message

C
O
N
G
R
A
T
U
L
A
T
I
O
N
S

You PowerWalked through...

Prayer Experiences
Observing 192 captivating stories
Worship Encounters
Exciting Sunday celebrations
Reading through 31 Proverbs and 17 Psalms
Writing down things for which you are grateful
Applying His story to your story
Learning 48 Scriptures
Keeping a journal to look back on for years to come

Time to celebrate! Invite some friends to celebrate with and tell them how you've grown in your walk with Christ. Encourage them to PowerWalk with Jesus this next year.

Write down what it means for you to finish PowerWalk.

Why I developed PowerWalk?

Simply put, I love teenagers. As a matter of fact, I love teens so much that I was one for seven whole years! After that I had four teens (they were kids first though).

Putting PowerWalk together was my way of helping teens combine their creative side with their desire to walk with God each day.

It is my sincere prayer that you grow in wonderful ways with your Lord and Savior, Jesus Christ. Thank you for powerwalking with Jesus.

Go to www.RodWhitlock.com to order additional copies of PowerWalk.